FIN RUNS

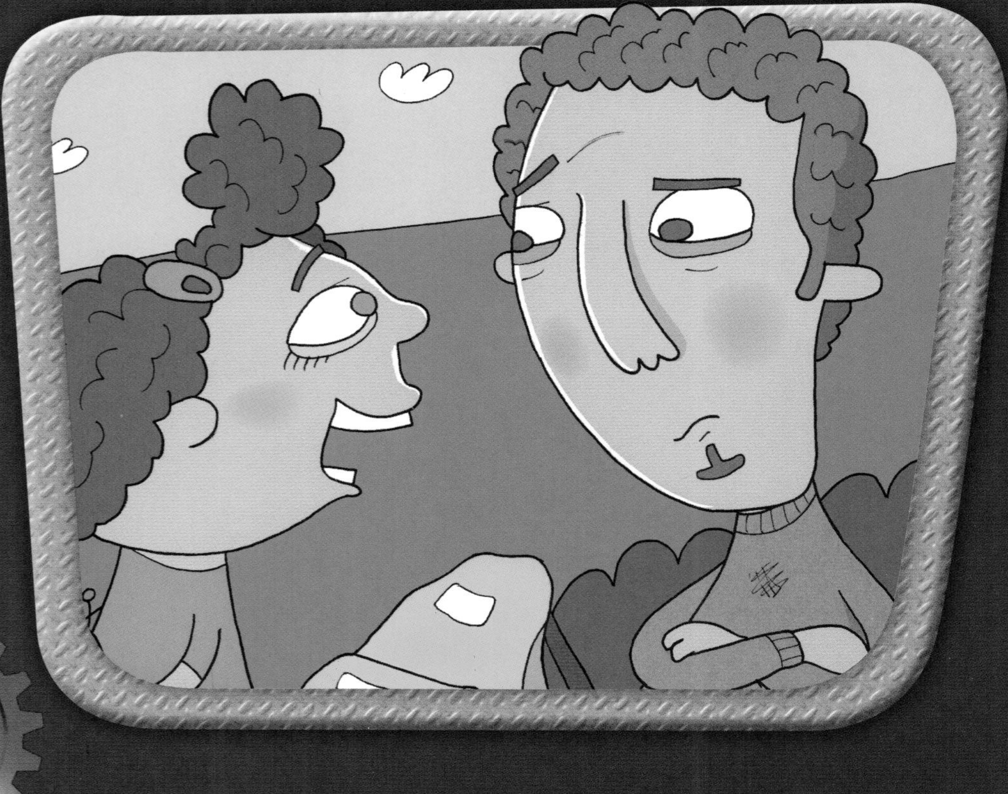

Written by Dale Tenby

Illustrated by The Boy Fitz Hammond

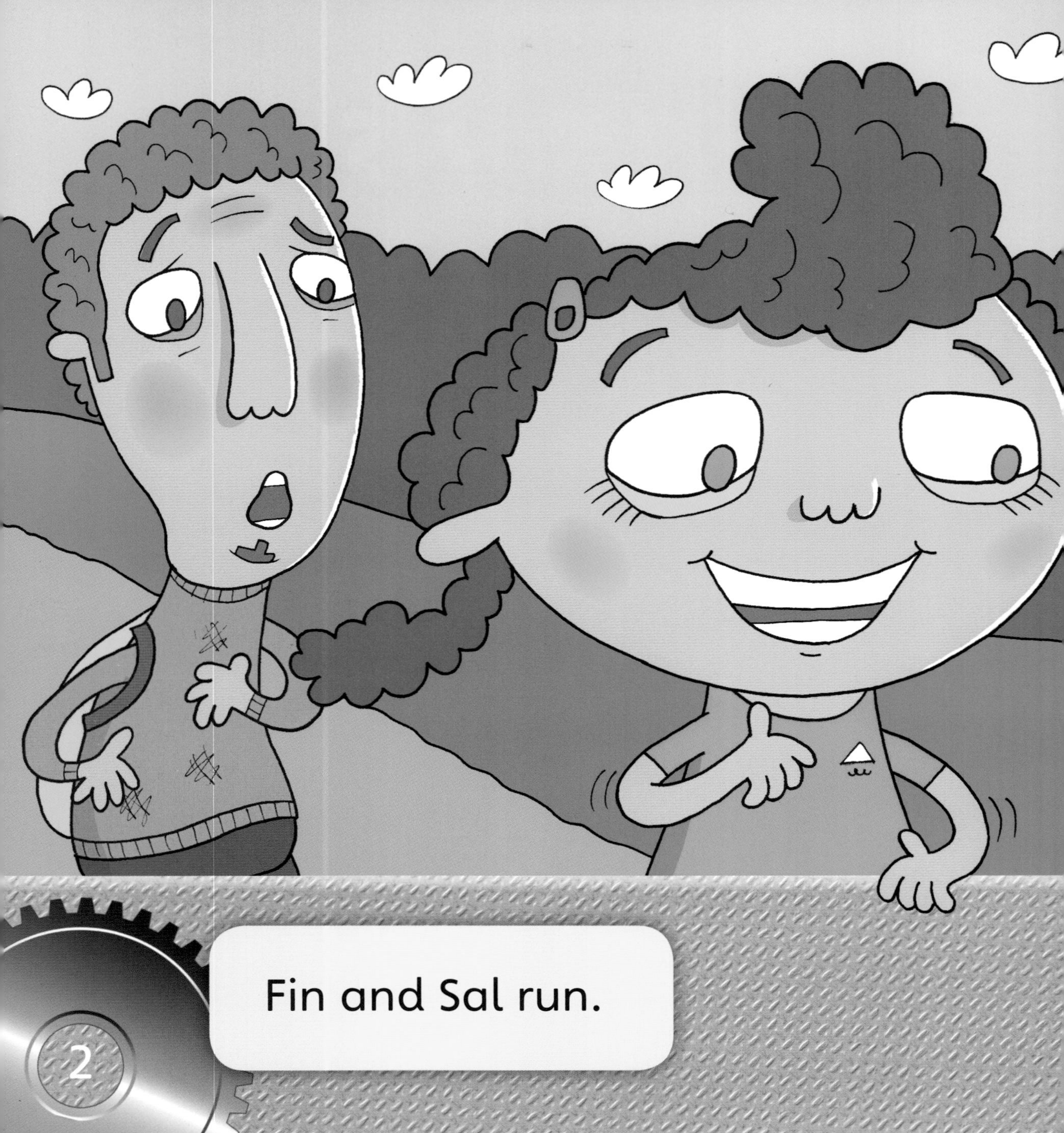

Fin and Sal run.

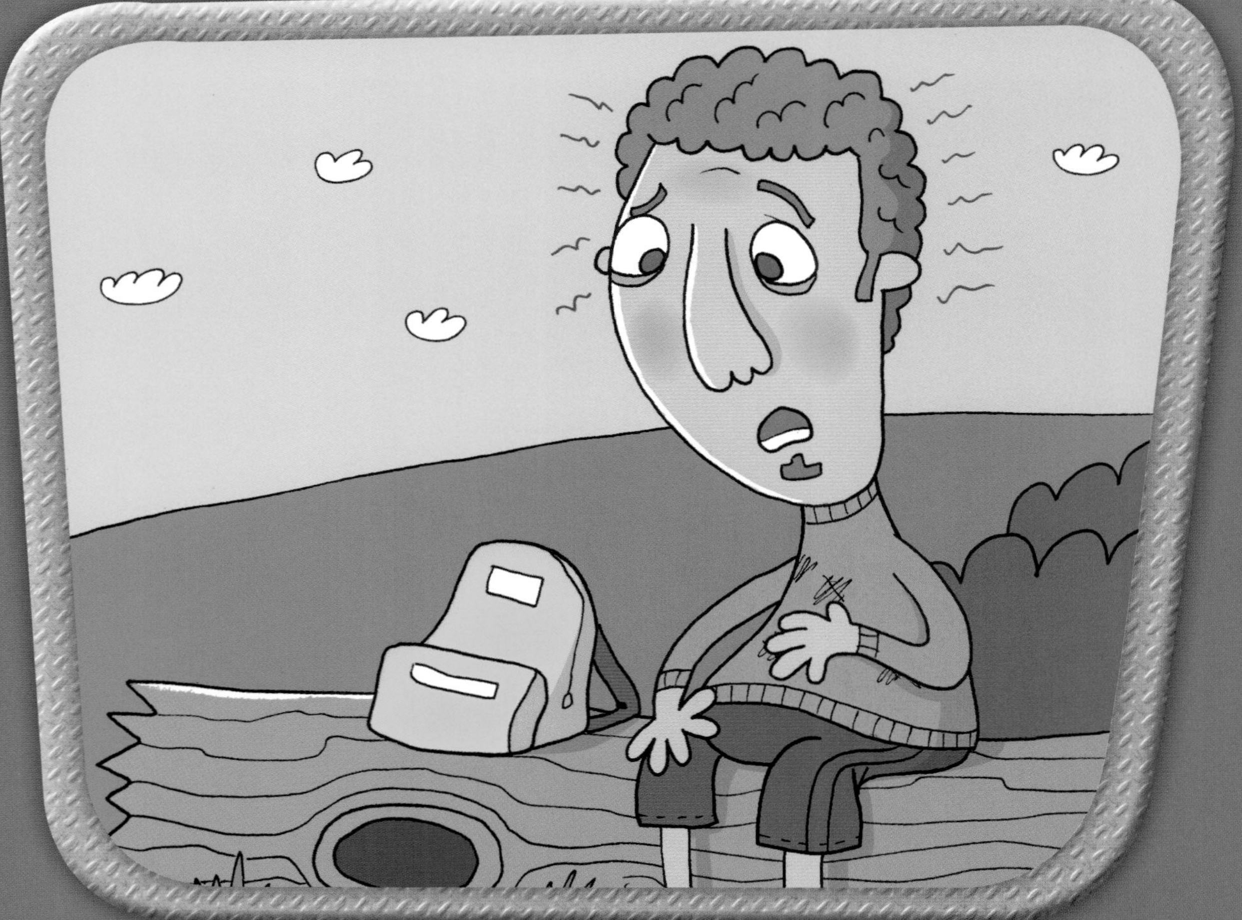

Fin sits on a log.
He can not run.

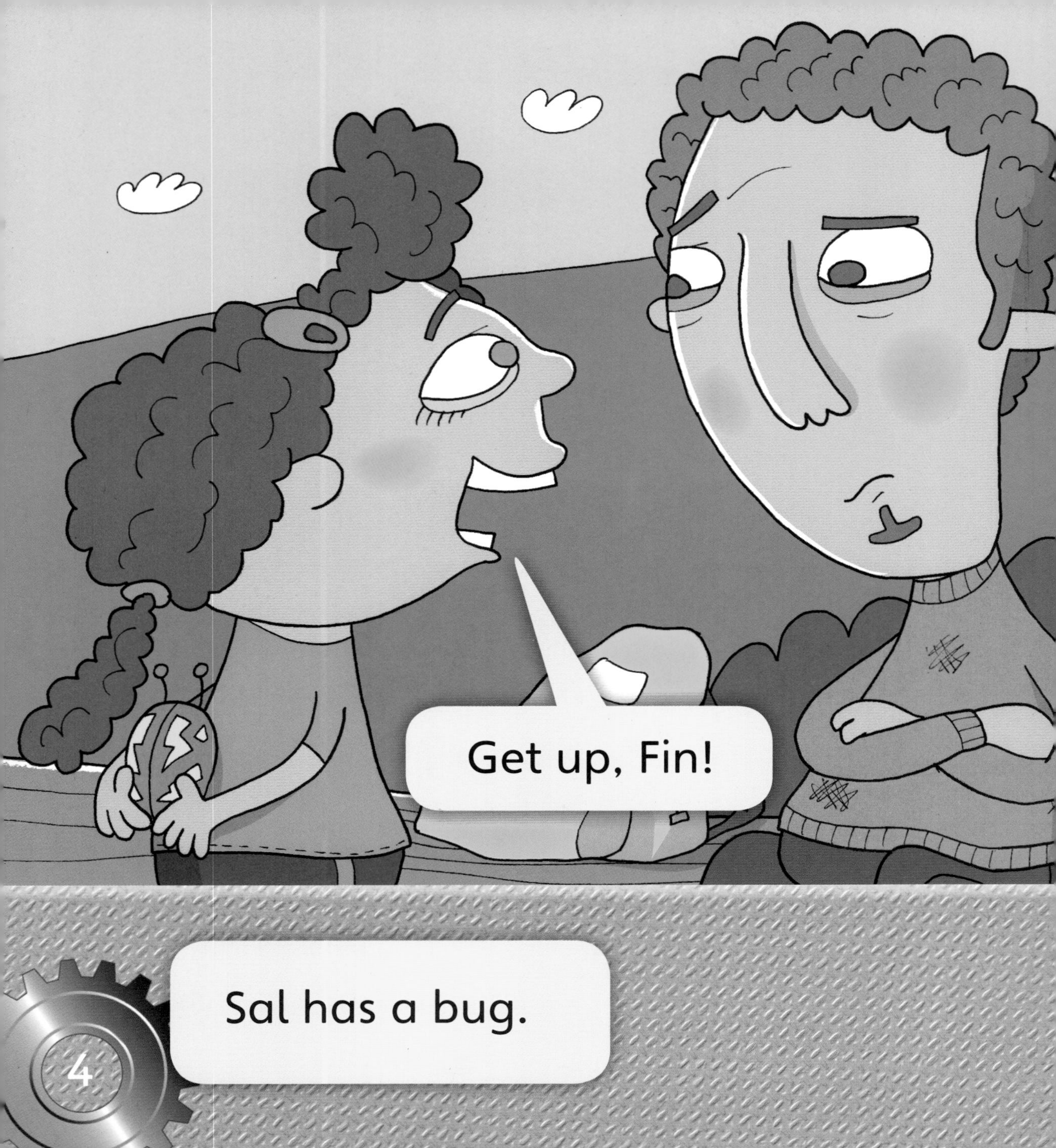
Get up, Fin!
Sal has a bug.

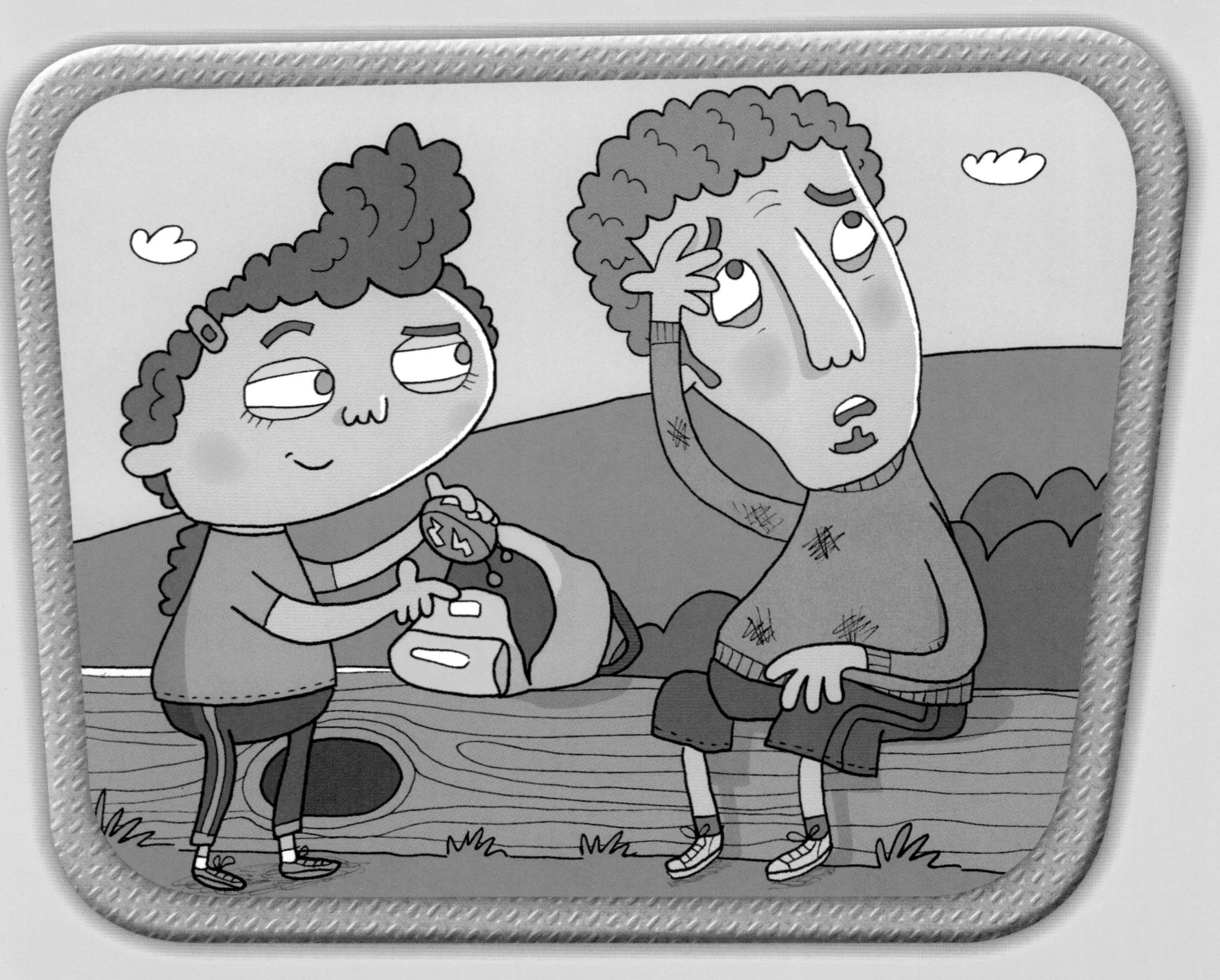

Sal pops the bug into Fin's bag.

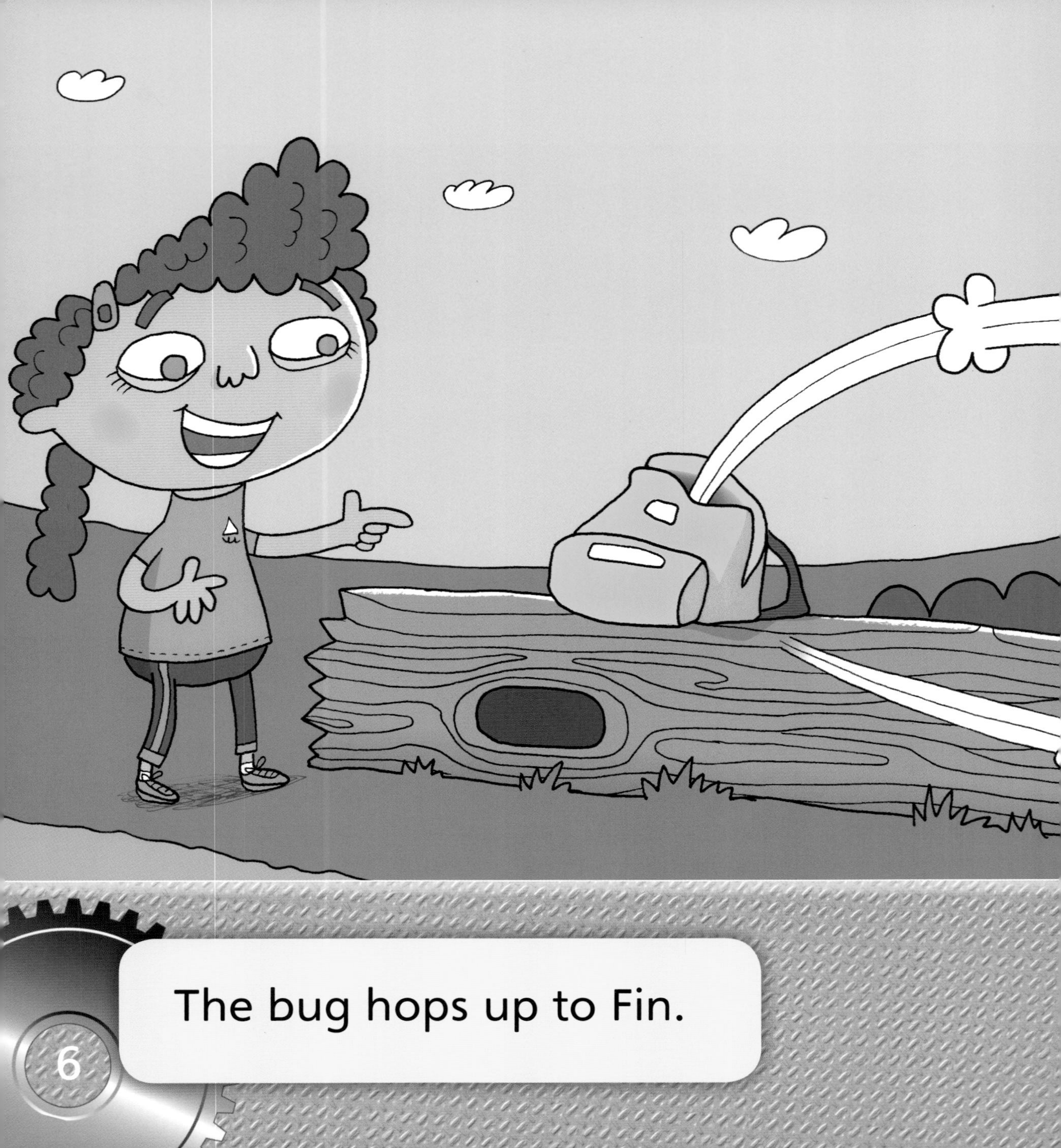

The bug hops up to Fin.

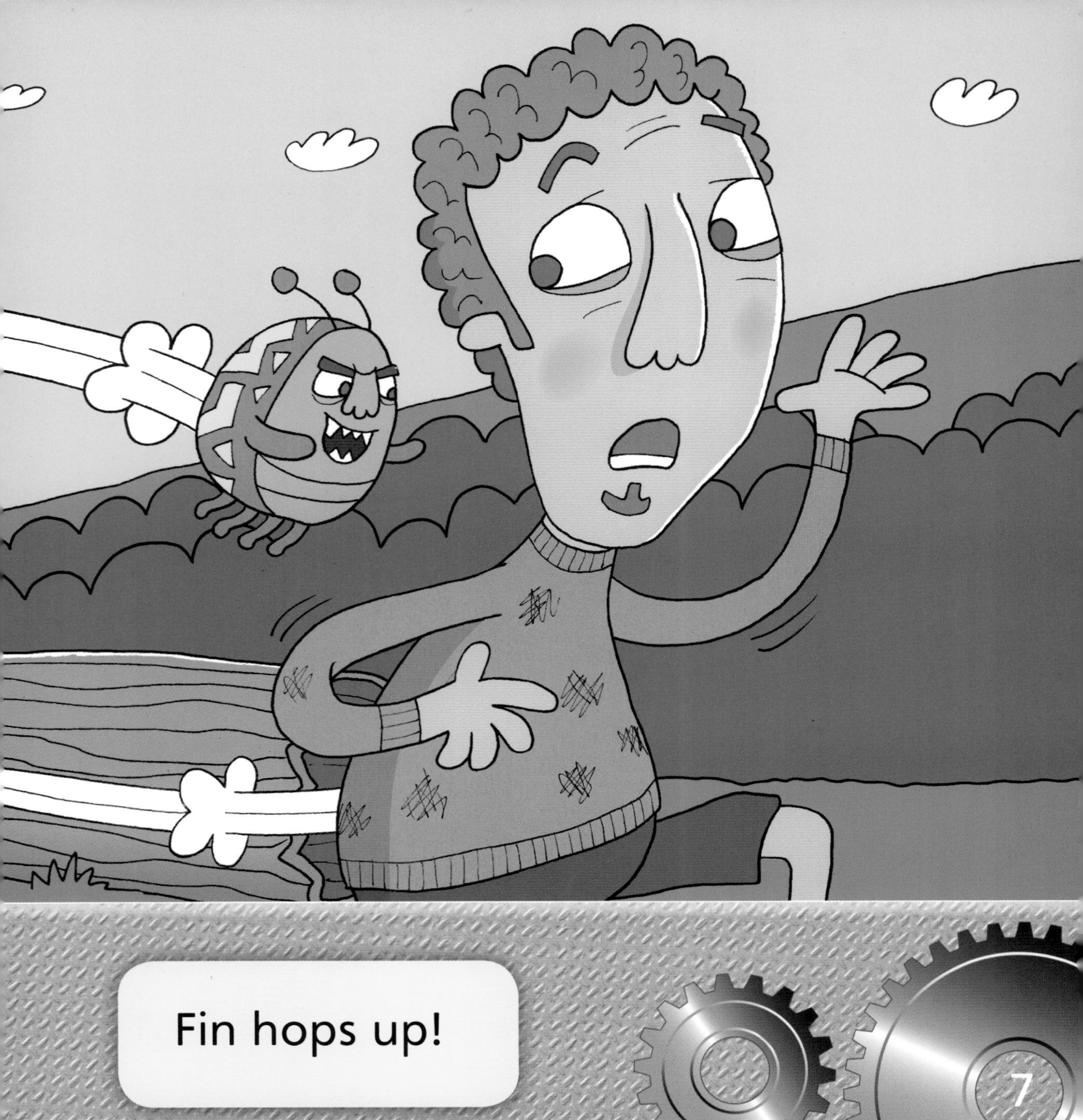

Fin hops up!

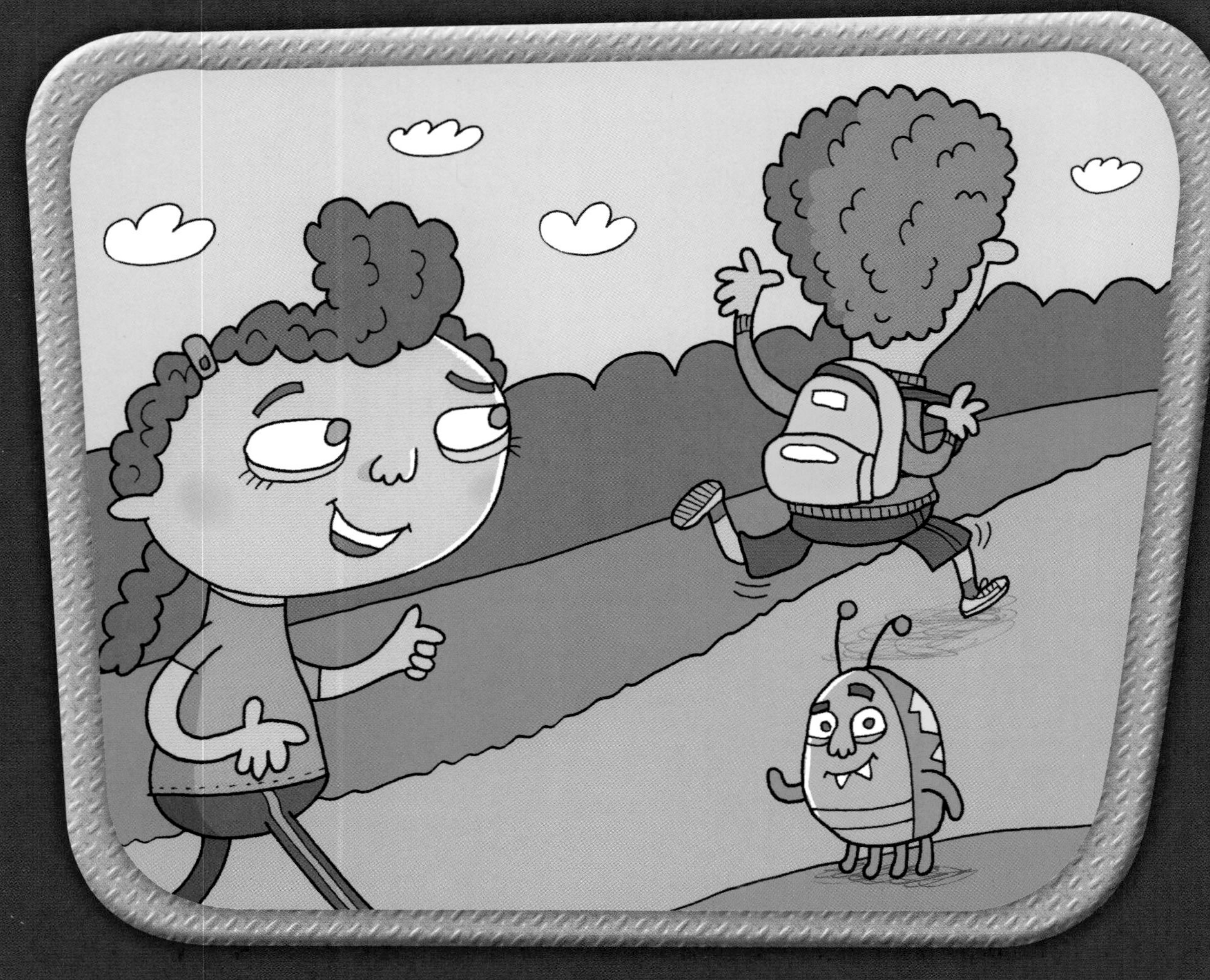

Fin runs. Sal runs.